CW00357862

THE MINIATURE BOOK OF

Christmas Crafts

a Salamander book

Published by Salamander Books Limited
LONDON • NEW YORK

A SALAMANDER BOOK

Published by Salamander Books Ltd
129-137 York Way
London N7 9LG

© Salamander Books Ltd 1992

ISBN 0 86101 723 4

Distributed in the United Kingdom by
Hodder & Stoughton Services
PO Box 6, Mill Road
Dunton Green, Sevenoaks
Kent TN13 2YA

All correspondence concerning the content of this volume
should be addressed to Salamander Books Ltd.

CREDITS

Projects by: *Suzie Major, Susy Smith and Rosalind Burdett*
Editor: *Lisa Dyer*
Photographer: *Steve Tanner and Terry Dilliway*
Designer: *Louise Bruce*
Filmset: *SX Composing Ltd*
Printed in Belgium

Contents

Satin 'Presents'

THESE PRETTY TREE
ORNAMENTS CAN BE MADE
ANY SIZE YOU DESIRE

1 For a cube shape, the pattern is a Latin cross (as shown). Make the long piece twice the length of the others and all other sides equal length. Cut this shape out in satin, then cut a piece of iron-on interfacing, 1cm (½in) smaller all around. Iron on the interfacing. Also iron in the creases to form the sides of the cube.

2 Placing right sides together, sew all the seams, using a small running stitch, cutting into the corners and using the interfacing edge as a seamline.

3 Leave one edge open so you can turn the cube right-side out. Stuff it with polyester filling, then slipstitch the opening edges together. Decorate the cube with ribbons and bows. For a rectangular box, simply widen the long section of the cross. The round box is a purchased box covered with satin.

Santa Faces

JOLLY FELT SANTA FACES
ADD CHRISTMAS CHEER
TO THE TREE

1 Using homemade cardboard templates, cut out all the separate pieces for the santa's face, hat, moustache, cheeks, mouth and nose in felt. Glue the main face piece to a piece of cardboard. When it is dry, cut around it.

2 All you have to do now is glue on all the other pieces. Affix the nose, mouth and cheeks before the moustache, which goes on top.

3 Place a loop of thread under the circle on the top of the hat, to hang the face on your Christmas tree. Glue on two darkly coloured sequins to represent the eyes.

Foliage Frame

ADD A FESTIVE TOUCH TO
A MIRROR OR PICTURE
WITH A FERNY FRAME

1 Make this unusual picture frame in separate sections, one horizontal and the other vertical. You need fake ivy, ferns and other foliage, plus pine cones, gold baubles and gold curling gift wrap ribbon. Cut off the long stems and wire individual pieces as shown, using florists' wire.

2 For the top section, gradually lay pieces on top of one another, binding the wires and stems together with tape as you go along. The arrangement should be long and narrow.

3 For the second section, use the same technique, but make the arrangement fuller. Then hold the two pieces as you would like them to sit on the frame, and wire them together. Bend the stem wires back so they will slip over the frame and hold the arrangement in place.

Everlasting Wreath

PLAITED TUBES OF FABRIC
MAKE A COLOURFUL RED
AND GREEN WREATH

1 For this project, you will need three strips of fabric in red, green and white, about 150cm (60in) long and 18cm (7in) wide. Sew them into tubes, right sides facing, leaving one end open. Turn each tube right-side out and stuff with polyester filling. Have a stick handy to help push the stuffing down the tube. Turn in the raw edges and sew closed.

2 Wind narrow red ribbon around the green tube, sewing it in place at each end to secure. When you have made all three tubes, plait them together loosely and join the ends together. Cover the point where they join with a large net bow and add three small net bows around the ring.

3 Thread tinsel through the wreath, and decorate with golden baubles, tied on with thread at the back. To finish, add some curly strands of gold gift wrap ribbon. Curl the ribbon by running the blunt edge of a pair of scissors along it.

Hoop-La!

HANG THIS TINSEL WREATH
ON A DOOR OR WALL FOR
HOLIDAY DECORATION

16

1 This Christmas wreath is based on a child's plastic hoop. First of all, buy a plastic hoop; any size will do. Cut long strips of wadding (batting) and wind them around the hoop, holding the edges in place with sticky tape. We gave it two layers of medium-weight wadding.

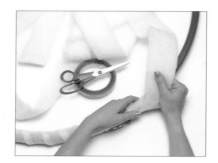

2 Next take some 8cm- (3in-) wide ribbon and wind it firmly around the hoop, in the opposite direction to the wadding. Make sure the wadding is entirely covered. Take a contrasting ribbon, about 6cm (2in) wide, and wrap it over the first, leaving equal spaces between the loops. Repeat with a third ribbon, 4cm (1½in) wide.

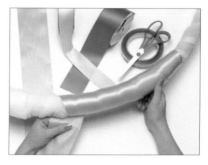

3 Make sure each ribbon starts and finishes in the same place so that all the joins are together. This will be the top of the hoop. Wind tinsel around the hoop, over the ribbons. Pin or staple a wide piece of ribbon over all the joins at the top. Tape a cluster of ribbon, tinsel, baubles and bells at the top and add a large bow.

Fancy Foil

SHINY RED FOIL BALLS
MAKE EFFECTIVE MOBILES
OR TREE ORNAMENTS

1 Cut out eight circles from foil wrapping paper in each of the following diameters: 9cm (3½in), 7.5cm (3in) and 6m (2¼in). Then cut out four cardboard circles 2cm (¾in) in diameter and two cardboard circles 1.5cm (½in) in diameter. Fold the largest foil circles into quarters and staple four of them on to a large cardboard circle.

2 In the same way, staple the other four foil circles to another cardboard circle. Glue the two cardboard circles together with a string between them. Leave a long piece hanging below for the other two balls. Fluff out the edges of foil to make a good shape.

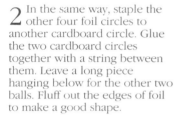

3 Now make the other two balls in the same way, using the smaller cardboard circles for the tiniest balls. Fix the balls to the string as you go.

Holiday Paperchains

BRIGHTLY COLOURED
TISSUE-PAPER CHAINS
ENLIVEN ANY PARTY

20

1 To make the circular chain, cut out two circles of cardboard 10cm (4in) in diameter, and lots of tissue paper circles the same size. Take ten tissue paper circles and fold in four. Now make two cuts as shown, from the single-folded edge almost to the double folds, then open out. Glue the centre of the first circle to the middle of one cardboard circle.

2 Next, take the second tissue circle and glue it to the first at the top and bottom. Glue the third circle to the centre of the second. Continue gluing alternate circles in the same place top and bottom. Finally glue the other cardboard circle to the last tissue circle to complete the paperchain.

3 For the flower chain, make two cardboard templates and cut out lots of shapes in coloured tissue paper. Dab a little glue on to every other petal of the first flower. Place the second flower on top. On the second flower, dab glue on alternate petals. Continue gluing in alternate positions until the chain is long enough. Glue the ends to the templates.

Christmas Trellis

A GOLD TRELLIS MAKES
A FESTIVE SETTING FOR A
CHRISTMAS CARD DISPLAY

1 Hanging up your Christmas cards always poses a problem. Here is a simple way to overcome the problem while making an interesting 'picture' for your wall at the same time. First take a piece of wooden garden trellis, extend it and spray it all over with gold paint.

2 While the trellis is drying, lay out some ordinary wooden clothes pegs (pins) and spray them gold as well. You will have to turn them over a few times so all the sides are covered.

3 When the trellis is dry, take some thick strands of tinsel and wind them all around the edge of the trellis to make a frame. Now hang the trellis on the wall, and use the pegs to attach cards as they arrive.

Golden Centrepiece

SPRAY FRUIT AND NUTS
WITH GOLD PAINT TO MAKE
A GLAMOROUS ARRANGEMENT

1 A touch of gold gives this platter of fruit and nuts extra richness. Begin by spraying ivy, clementines, bay leaves and fir cones with gold paint. If the fruit will be eaten, make sure that the paint you are using is non-toxic.

2 Place the ivy leaves around the edge of a plain oval platter. The flatter the plate, the better, for this will allow the ivy leaves to hang over the edge.

3 Arrange the clementines on the platter, surround them with dates and nuts, and place a bunch of shiny black grapes on top. Add the gold leaves and fir cones for a luxurious finishing touch to the arrangement.

Frosted Fruit

A PLATE OF SUGAR-FROSTED
FRUIT MAKES AN ELEGANT
WINTER-TIME CENTREPIECE

1 This stunning centrepiece looks grand enough to grace the most formal Christmas dinner table, and yet it is very simple to make. Choose a selection of fresh fruit, and, using a pastry brush, coat each piece of fruit with egg white.

2 Working over a large plate, sprinkle granulated sugar over the fruit so that it adheres to the egg coating. Alternatively, the fruit can be dipped into a bowl of sugar, although this tends to make the sugar lumpy.

3 Ivy leaves are used to form a decorative border around the plate; but remember to use a doily to separate the poisonous leaves from the fruit if you intend to eat the fruit later.

Glitter Tree Mat

MAKE A CHRISTMAS MEAL
SPECIAL WITH SPARKLING
TREE PLACEMATS

1 This sparkling placemat is an obvious winner for Christmas. First draw a Christmas tree on the reverse (matt) side of a piece of shiny green cardboard. The length should be about 10cm (4in) longer than the diameter of your dinner plate and the width about 20cm (8in) wider. Cut out the mat using a craft knife and a steel ruler.

2 Add 'ornaments' by sticking tiny baubles to the tips of the tree using strong glue. Then cut out or buy a star shape to put at the top of the tree.

3 Finally, stick small silver stars over the mat. Or, if you prefer, just scatter the stars freely over the mat, first placing each mat on the table in position.

Butterfly Napkin

A SIMPLE BUT ELEGANT
NAPKIN FOLD ENHANCES ANY
CHRISTMAS TABLE

1 A crisply starched napkin is required for this pretty fold. Lay the napkin flat. Fold two edges to meet in the centre as shown. Then fold the half nearest you across the centre line and over on top of the other half, to form a long rectangle.

2 Fold the right-hand end of the rectangle in towards the centre, and with another fold double it back on itself as shown. Repeat with the left-hand side so the double folds meet in the centre.

3 Pull the right-hand back corner across to the left, bringing the front edge across the centre line to form a triangle. Anchoring the right-hand side of the triangle with one hand, use the other hand to fold the corner back to its original position, thus creating the 'wings' of the arrangement. Repeat the process on the left-hand side.

Holly Wreath

HANG THIS EVERLASTING
WREATH ON THE DOOR AS A
WARM WELCOME TO GUESTS

1 Cut 5cm (2in) squares of green crepe paper and stick a small piece of masking tape in the centre for extra strength. Cut the point off a cocktail stick and use it to make holes in a polystyrene ring. Push each square into a hole with the blunt end of the stick.

2 Continue pushing in squares until the ring is hidden. Take some artificial red berries on wires and push them into the wreath at random to decorate.

3 Tie a large bow of red satin ribbon. Bend a length of wire into a 'U' shape and thread through the back of the bow. Push the ends of the wire into the wreath.

Forest Foliage

DRESS UP A SIDEBOARD
OR TABLE WITH THIS FIERY
RED CANDLE ARRANGEMENT

1 This arrangement is bright and cheery and the materials are quite easy to find. If you do not have woodland nearby, your florist should have sections of bark for sale. Also, buy a plastic candle holder. Put a large lump of green Plasticine (modelling clay) on the bark, and insert your candle holder on top.

2 Now take some plastic or silk fern and spray it gold. Break off pieces when it is dry, and stick them into the Plasticine. Also wire up strands of red paper ribbon, pine cones and red baubles, and insert these.

3 When the Plasticine is artistically concealed, put the candle in the holder, and set the arrangement on a sideboard or table. Put a mat under it, or it will scratch the surface.

Ivy Candle Ring

AN IVY CENTREPIECE
BRINGS DARK EVERGREEN
COLOUR TO THE TABLE

1 This elegant candle ring is the ideal centrepiece for a Christmas dinner party. A circular cake base serves as the foundation for the arrangement. Begin by attaching strands of ivy to the edge of the base, securing them with drawing pins (tacks).

2 Build up the ring by adding more strands and bunches of leaves until only a small space remains in the centre. Push stems of freesia among the ivy leaves to provide a striking colour contrast.

3 Use a mixture of white and green candles of varying heights to form the centre of the arrangement. Secure each candle to the base with a blob of glue or modelling clay.

Festive Miniatures

MINIATURE DRIED
ARRANGEMENTS MAKE PRETTY
NOVELTIES FOR THE TREE

1 One of these pretty ornaments is made with cinnamon sticks. Take three sticks and bind them together with wire. Wire on a double bow made with gold gift wrap ribbon, and then add a posy of cones and small red helichrysum (strawflower or everlasting).

2 To make the other arrangement, first spray a small basket and a few walnuts with gold paint. When these are dry, fill the basket with a block of florists' foam. Pack the foam with gold South African daisies (a type of helichrysum) to form a spherical shape.

3 Push a length of wire through one end of each of the walnuts. Insert three or four nuts into the display, pushing them deep down amongst the flowers. Wire a small bow and attach it to the handle. Finally, attach a loop of gold cord to each arrangement so you can hang the ornament.

Noël Place Marker

MAKE PASTRY MARKERS
IN CHRISTMAS SHAPES OF
TREES, BELLS OR STARS

1 This pastry place marker is made using a simple dough. Mix three parts of white flour to one of salt, a spoonful of glycerine and enough cold water to give a good consistency. Knead the pastry for about 10 minutes, then roll it flat on a floured surface.

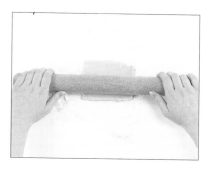

2 Cut out the Christmas tree shape with a sharp knife or pastry cutter. Remember to make a hole for the ribbon. Bake the pastry in the normal way.

3 Colour the tree green with a water-based paint. You can pipe a Christmas message or your guest's name on the tree using tube paint. Varnish the tree and attach a ribbon. These pastry shapes are not edible and should be used for decorative purposes only; however they can be used year after year.

Twinkling Stars

HANG FOIL STARS FROM
THE WALLS OR CEILING TO
DECORATE YOUR HOME

1 First make a pattern for the star using a ruler and protractor. Draw an equilaterial triangle (each angle is 60°) on a piece of cardboard. Cut out the triangle and use it as a pattern to make another one. Then glue one triangle over the other to form the star. Use this pattern to cut a star from foil paper.

2 Fold the foil star in half three times between opposite points. Next fold it in half three times between opposite angles, as shown. Every angle and point should have a fold in it.

3 The star will now easily bend into its sculptured shape. Make a small hole in its top point with a hole punch or skewer, then put some strong thread through the hole to hang the star up.

Highland Holly

MAKE AN ATTRACTIVE HOLLY
GARLAND WITH GREEN FLET
AND TARTAN RIBBON

1 Deck the halls with sprigs of holly made from felt and suspended from tartan ribbon. Make a holly pattern or template from paper and cut out two pieces of green felt and one of wadding (batting) for every sprig. Place the two felt pieces together, with wadding in between, and pin in place. Overstitch all around the edges with embroidery thread.

2 Thread your sewing machine with green cotton thread and stitch 'veins' on each holly leaf – one down the centre and the rest sloping from the centre to the points. Next, take four red wooden or plastic beads for each leaf and sew them in place, close to the inside edge of the leaf, using six strands of red embroidery thread.

3 Measure a length of tartan ribbon from which to hang the holly. Now cut shorter lengths to make the bows. Tie the sprigs to the garland with the short ribbons. Finish off with a bow. Finally, cut a 'V' in the tails of the bows and hang your garland in place.